Christchurch Mass

A Setting for Soprano Voices

Malcolm Archer

Kevin Mayhew

We hope you enjoy *Christchurch Mass.*
Further copies are available from your local music shop
or Christian bookshop.

In case of difficulty, please contact the publisher direct by writing to:

The Sales Department
KEVIN MAYHEW LTD
Rattlesden
Bury St Edmunds
Suffolk
IP30 0SZ

Phone 0449 737978
Fax 0449 737834

Please ask for our complete catalogue of outstanding Church Music.

Front Cover: *Byzantine Icon of St Gregory.*
Pushkin Museum, Moscow/Bridgeman Art Library, London.
Reproduced by kind permission.

First published in Great Britain in 1992 by Kevin Mayhew Ltd.

© Copyright 1992 by Kevin Mayhew Ltd.

ISBN 0 86209 350 3

Cover designed by Juliette Clarke and Graham Johnstone.
Picture Research: Jane Rayson.
Music Editor: Joanne Clarke.

Printed and bound in Great Britain.

For Martin Schellenberg and the Choir of Christchurch Priory, Dorset.

CHRISTCHURCH MASS

Malcolm Archer (b.1952)

KYRIE

3

Ky - ri - e, Ky - ri - e,

Ky - ri - e, e - lei - son,

Chri - ste, e - lei - son,

Chri - ste, e - lei - son,

Chri - ste, Chri - ste,

Chri - ste, e - le - i - son.

5

Ky - ri - e, e - lei - son. Ky - ri -

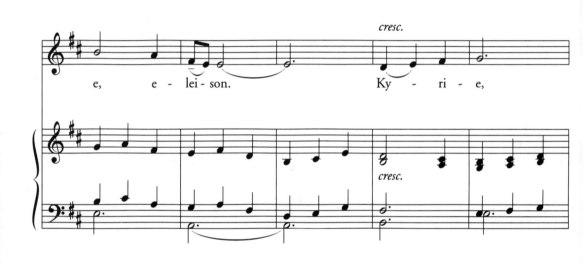

e, e - lei - son. Ky - ri - e,

cresc.

cresc.

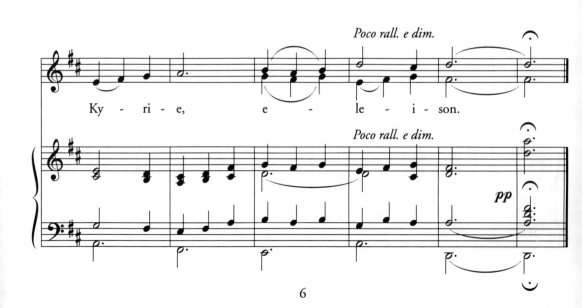

Poco rall. e dim.

Ky - ri - e, e - le - i - son.

Poco rall. e dim.

pp

6

GLORIA

te.   A-do - ra   -   mus te.   Glo-ri-fi - ca   -   mus

te.   Gra - ti- as   a - gi-mus ti- bi prop- ter

+Gt. to ped.

mag- nam glo-ri- am tu - am.   Do - mi-ne De - us,

Soprano 1

mp legato

Sw.

Gt. to ped.

8

9

10

Qui tol - lis pec - ca - ta mun - di, mi - se - re - re

no - bis.

Qui tol - lis pec - ca - ta mun - di,

su - sci - pe de - pre - ca - ti - o - nem no - stram.

Man.

Gt. or Ch.

Qui se-des ad dex-te-ram Pa-tris, mi-se-re-re no - bis.

Sw. *mf cresc.*

Ped.

Quo - ni - am tu so - lus sanc - tus,

Gt. *f*

+ Gt. to Ped.

tu so - lus sanc - tus. Tu so - lus Do - mi-

Tu

Sw.

– Gt. to Ped.

13

Cum Sanc - to Spi - ri - tu, in glo - ri - a De - i

Pa - tris. A - men, A - men, A - men.

poco rall.

SANCTUS

ter - ra glo-ri - a tu - a, Ho-san - na in ex - cel - sis, Ho-

ter - ra glo-ri - a tu - a, Ho-san - na in ex -

san - na in ex - cel - sis, Ho-san - na, Ho-

cel - sis. Ho - san - na in ex - cel - sis, Ho-san -

san - na, Ho-san - na in ex - cel - sis!

na, Ho-san - na,Ho-san - na in ex - cel - sis!

BENEDICTUS

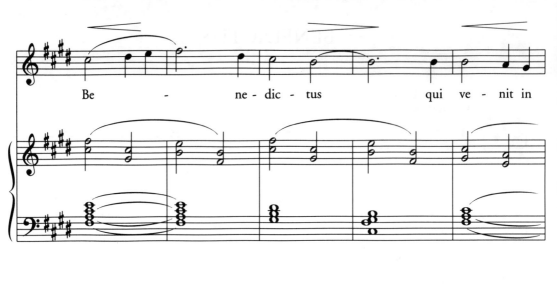

Be - - - ne - dic - tus qui ve - nit in

no - mi - ne Do - mi-ni, in no - mi-ne Do - mi-

Tempo di Hosanna

ni. Ho - san - na in ex - cel - sis, Ho-

Ho - san - na in ex -

Gt.

18

san - na in ex - cel - sis, Ho - san - na, Ho-

cel - sis, Ho - san - na in ex - cel - sis, Ho-san -

san - na, Ho-san - na in ex - cel - sis.

na, Ho-san - na, Ho-san - na in ex - cel - sis.

rall.

AGNUS DEI

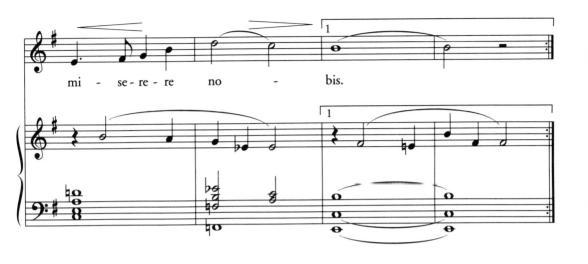

mi – se-re-re no – bis.

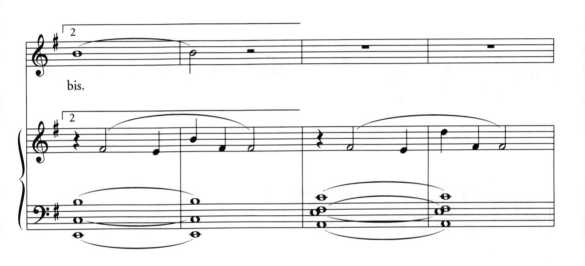

bis.

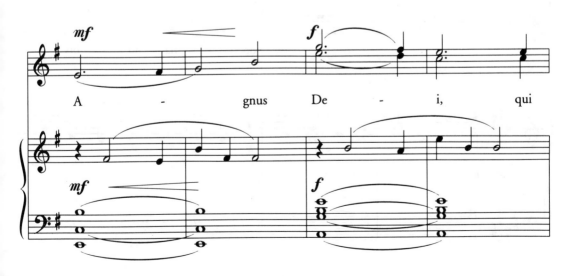

A – gnus De – i, qui

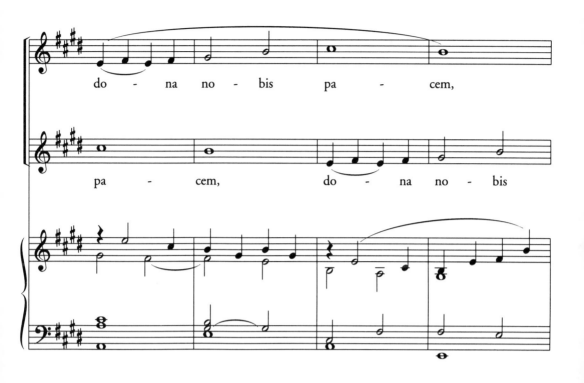

do - na no - bis pa - cem,

pa - cem, do - na no - bis

do - na, do - na no - bis pa - cem.

pa - cem, no - bis pa - cem.

GW01218023

THE ESSENTIAL MEDITERRANEAN DIET COOKBOOK

Simple, Healthy Recipes for Beginners and Pros incl. 3 Weeks Weight Loss Plan

[1st Edition]

Matthew K. Williams

ISBN- 9798656867108

TABLE OF CONTENTS

Part 1
Introduction

Mediterranean diet

The Mediterranean diet is a diet plan that contains many vegetables, fruits, whole grains, fish and olive oil. The Mediterranean diet reduces the risk of certain cancers, cardiovascular disease, diabetes, Alzheimer's and Parkinson's diseases. If you want to lose the weight, this diet will be great for that.

An American physiologist Ancel Keys was the first one who starts to popularize this type of diet. He discovered that people of Crete and southern Italy have a better cardiovascular system than US citizens. They ate fresh foods mainly of vegetable origin and engaged in physical labor. Speaking of the diet of Mediterranean area, one must understand that this is the traditional diet of the Mediterranean countries, not its modern "restaurant" version.

There is no clear list of products that the Mediterranean diet includes. This is an indicative healthy eating plan that can be adjusted to suit your own taste and preferences. The Mediterranean cuisines are very diverse, but they all share the following principles:

1) Mostly vegetable food (fruits and vegetables; pasta, cereals and whole-grain bread; legumes and nuts);

2) Olive oil instead of butter; Will be good extra-virgin olive oil.

3) Use of spices and herbs instead of salt to improve the taste of food;

4) Reduced consumption of red meat up to 1-2 times per month;

5) Include fish and bird 2 times a week;

6) The moderate use of wine;

7) Sufficient physical activity and active way of life.

The Mediterranean diet is represented as a food pyramid. The pyramid is based on fruits, vegetables, nuts, pasta, bread and cereals. Every day, everyone should eat at least 5 servings of fruits and vegetables. It is better to avoid white bread and rice. In case they use bread, it should be whole grain and the only adding is olive oil.

Nuts are an integral part of the Mediterranean diet. Due to the high-calories they have, it is advisable to eat no more than a handful in one hand per day. The Mediterranean diet also contains many legumes. Try to gradually introduce in your diet beans, chickpeas, peas and lentils. They can be used to prepare soups and other dishes.

The main source of fat is the olive in the Mediterranean diet. It includes a lot of monounsaturated fats. If you replace the saturated fats (butter, meat, etc.) with olive oil, the body will reduce the level of "bad" cholesterol which is low-density lipoproteins. It is better to use extra-virgin and virgin olive oil that has undergone the smallest processing. It contains maximum antioxidants.

The Mediterranean diet cannot be imagined without fish and seafood. Oily fish (mackerel, rainbow trout, sardines, salmon, herring) is rich in omega-3 fatty acids, beneficial for skin and cardiovascular health. The Mediterranean diet involves moderate consumption of eggs and dairy products, for example, cheese and yogurt. Preferably consume yogurts made from skim milk and low-fat cheeses such as mozzarella, feta and halum. Yogurt is also oily. It is good idea to choose foods that are low in fat. Red meat appears on the table only 1-2 times a month. It is not an everyday meal, but rather a delicacy that you can rarely indulge yourself with.

Some scientific studies indicate that moderate wine consumption makes the risk of heart disease less. But it is good to understand what is "moderate use". For women, it is 150 ml (1 glass) of wine and for men, it is 300 ml (2 glasses) a day. In this case, the daily dose can not be "accumulated". If you have not been drinking all week, this does not mean that you can empty the entire bottle on weekends.

Despite the caloric content of olive oil, the Mediterranean diet is one of the most correct and useful eating styles. Enriched with fiber, omega 3 fats and protein.

How to start the diet?

Here are 7 simple things to start the diet.

1) A big quantity of vegetables. Starting with a simple plate of sliced fresh tomatoes drizzled with olive oil and pieces of feta cheese to stunning salads, different stews and soups, healthy pizzas, garlicky greens or oven-roasted medleys. Vegetables are a very important ingredient in the Mediterranean kitchen and special diet.

2) Less meat. There is a super way to change your mind about the meat. Wild meat is better and much healthier then the meat you use to buy at supermarkets. But there is no way and no need to hunt each day. Just use the meat twice a month but check the quality you have. This way you will help not only your health but also the environment as the meat industry is one of the largest and most harmful for nature.

3) Dairy products. There are different types of cheese and yogurts now. Try to discover new tastes.

4) Seafood. You need to use fish. For example tuna, salmon and herring are rich in omega 3. The similar effect but for heart and brains have shellfish, oysters, mussels and dams.

5) Quality fats. You need to include extra-virgin olive oil, peanuts, olives, a variety of nuts and avocados.

6) Whole grains. They include many important nutrients, also their nuttier taste, fuller and fiber will keep you comfortable with your stomach for a few hours. The gains like farro, bulgur, favor, barley, black and red rice are good traditional Mediterranean products which you can easily cook at home.

7) Fresh fruits. The main thing in the question of the desert is no sugar. Basically, you will be happy after you will stop using it. So instead of cookies and ice cream try some fresh juice or a new type of fruit you have never try before.

Loose up to 21 kilos per 3 weeks

Japanese researchers presented another study that found a link between eating speed and body mass index and waist circumference. The Mediterranean diet, which consist of lots of vegetables, fish and other healthy foods, has been discovered to be especially beneficial for women. This is evidenced by data from a new study of postmenopausal patients in Brazil, writes Medical Express. Researchers reported higher bone and muscle mass in menopausal women who followed the Mediterranean diet than those who did not. In particular, the Mediterranean diet successfully prevents cardiovascular disease, cancer and diabetes. It ranks second in the US ranking of the best diets for healthy eating since the 38th.

One of the most popular diets is a technique that combines a series of fasting days. The main thing is that it is easy to use it and it gives good results. It all depends on how honest you are in front of yourself and whether you break the rules of the diet or not.

Here are some bits of advice bout how to lose weight fast:

✓ 1-2 kilo dropping per week is a healthy weight loss. It is possible to make it more but it will be unsafe and in general, you are going just to lose muscle mass and store more fat. If to transfer that to calories, one kilo is 7700 calories, which means, you need to burn 1100 calories in order to lose 1 kilo in a week.

✓ You do not need to feel hungry all the time. You need to feel full all day. Otherwise, your motivation will fall down. So, if you need it, you can eat six times per day instead of two or three, but make your portions less.

✓ Combine cardio and strength training. You do not need to stay all day in the sports complex. Just one hour of running, swimming or cycling.

✓ You need to keep track of your fat, protein, calories, carbohydrates and physical activities. Make sure your water level is good. Moreover, good hydrating will make your skin glow and stay young longer.

✓ Forget about junk food. There is no way you lose your weight staying with hamburgers or any other fast food. If you see some healthy snacks, check if there is no sugar and start to read the labels of the products you buy.

✓ Take out 500 calories from your daily menu. And mind that sometimes it is enough to take a glass of water to feel full again for the next half an hour.

The advantage of the Mediterranean diet is that it includes different product groups, making it easy, combining products from different groups: vegetables, fruits, meat, fish, poultry, dairy products, whole grains, legumes, nuts, herbs, spices.

On a five-point scale, short-term weight loss in the Mediterranean diet is estimated at 3.4 points, and long-term - 3.2 points. To follow a diet is easy - this figure is estimated at 3.7 points. And for health it is very useful - the benefit of experts is estimated at 4.7 points on a five-point scale.

Part 2
Recipes

BREAKFAST

It is believed that a proper breakfast should contain carbohydrate food, since during the day energy is actively consumed and excess calories do not contribute to the deposition of body fat. No need to be lazy and save time when preparing breakfast. The breakfast menu includes omelets made with egg white, ricotta cheese, as well as whole-grain bread toasts (without bran screening) and peanut butter.

Fruit and nut granola

Servings: 8 | Total Time: 60 mins

Nutrition Information

Calories: 467 | Carbs: 64.2 grams | Fats: 20.7 grams

Ingredients:

- Nuts150 g
- Oatmeal 300 g
- Peeled Pumpkin Seeds 50 g
- Honey 150 g
- Olive oil 60 ml
- Apple Juice125 ml
- Ground cinnamon to taste
- Dried Cherries100 g
- Flax seeds to taste
- Raisins 100 g

Instructions:

1. Chop nuts (I took walnuts and cashews). Mix in a bowl with oatmeal and seeds (your choice). It is better to take cereals that cook for at least 10-15 minutes (!)

2. Mix honey, juice, oil and cinnamon in the saucepan. Put on the fire and, stirring, wait until all the ingredients are combined (you do not need to boil).

3. Pour liquid into dry ingredients and mix well.

4. Put in a mold and bake for 50-60 minutes at 160 degrees. Pour out and mix well every 8-10 minutes so that the granola does not burn and evenly bakes.

5. While granola is baked, cut dried fruits (in my case, dried cherries and raisins)

6. After the granola is cooked, let it cool.

7. Add dried fruits and fried sesame to the cooled granola (you can not add it to anyone you like) and mix everything well.

8. You can eat with milk and fresh fruits, with yogurt.

9. Granola is stored in a closed jar for several weeks.

Delicate omelet with toast by Gordon Ramsay

Servings: 2 | Total Time: 10 mins

Nutrition Information
Calories: 275 | Carbs: 10 grams | Fats: 21.1 grams

Ingredients:

- Chicken egg 2 pieces
- Butter 20 g
- Curd cheese 3 tablespoons
- Salt and ground black pepper to taste
- Rye bread 2 slices

Instructions:

1. Melt the butter in a not big saucepan. Beat the eggs and pour them into the stew pan, mix with oil. Stir it constantly over medium heat to prevent the mixture from solidifying from below. Add cottage cheese and mix thoroughly to allow the cheese to dissolve.

2. When the mixture begins to thicken, remove the saucepan from the heat and continue stirring, the eggs will continue to set, thanks to the heated bottom. Add salt and pepper, and, if desired, seasonings to your taste or fresh herbs. If necessary, return the pan to the fire. Stir until the mass is thick enough, but still maintain a delicate, creamy consistency.

3. Toast bread in a pan or in a toaster at the same time. Serve toasts with eggs laid on top, add fried champions, tomatoes or canned beans if desired.

Pate with smoked salmon and dill

Servings: 4 | Total Time: 30 mins

Nutrition Information

Calories: 286 | Carbs: 3.2 grams | Fats: 26.3 grams

Ingredients:

- Dill 2 tablespoons
- Mascarpone Cheese 230 g
- Lemon juice 1 tablespoon
- Smoked Salmon115 g
- Salt and ground black pepper to taste

Instructions:

1. Mix mascarpone in a blender, finely chopped dill and juice of lemon. Add half the finely chopped salmon and chop until smooth.

2. Transfer to a bowl and add the remaining.

3. Use salt and pepper due to your taste.

Fruit breakfast with nuts

Servings: 2 | Total Time: 10 mins

Nutrition Information

Calories: 1043 | Carbs: 62.2 grams | Fats: 82.1 grams

Ingredients:

- 🍽 Bananas 2 pieces
- 🍽 Walnuts 250 g
- 🍽 Apple 1 piece

Instructions:

1. Cut the apple into small pieces like cubes.

2. Crush the peeled nuts, mix with an apple.

3. Grind the banana in a blender and pour apples with nuts.

Frittata with broccoli and sweet pepper

Frittata with broccoli and sweet pepper is a classic Italian omelet. The main ingredient here is not eggs, but coarsely chopped vegetables, so there should be a lot of them. The eggs only fix the structure. It turns out a voluminous, embossed and beautiful dish.

Servings: 4 | Total Time: 16 mins

Nutrition Information

Calories: 377 | Carbs: 13.7 grams | Fats: 28.8 grams

Ingredients:

- 6 eggs
- Sweet pepper 3 pieces
- Red onion 1 head
- Broccoli Cabbage 150 g
- Parsley 20 g
- Olive oil 50 ml
- 2 cloves of garlic
- Lemon ¼ pieces
- Butter 30 g
- Nutmeg to taste
- Paprika to taste
- Thyme 1 bunch
- Salt to taste
- Ground black pepper to taste

Instructions:

1. Mix eggs with salt, ground nutmeg and paprika.

2. Dismantle the broccoli into inflorescence, peel the peppers and cut into thin strips. Cut the onion into thin half rings.

3. Chop the garlic and parsley, mix them with lemon juice and olive oil.

4. Fry the chopped onion in butter until soft, add broccoli, fry for a minute, then send pepper there, fry for another minute, add a pinch of thyme leaves, a minute later parsley with garlic in lemon juice and oil, and pour eggs in thirty seconds.

5. When the eggs begin to harden, send the pan to the oven preheated to 180 degrees for seven to ten minutes. Serve with salt, pepper and sprinkled with thyme leaves.

Meals with meat

The Mediterranean diet, combined with lean red meat, has cardiometabolic benefits for overweight or obese adults. There are few recipes of meat in this section.

Guinea fowl with spicy quinoa pilaf

Servings: 6 | Total Time: 90 mins

Nutrition Information

Calories: 645 | Carbs: 35.8 grams | Fats: 24.9 grams

Ingredients:

- 🍽 Anise (star anise) 2 pieces
- 🍽 Guinea fowl 1.5 kg
- 🍽 Quinoa300 g
- 🍽 Butter 50 g
- 🍽 Vegetable oil50 ml
- 🍽 Dry white wine100 ml
- 🍽 Lime 2 pieces
- 🍽 Green chili pepper 1 piece
- 🍽 Onion 1 head
- 🍽 Garlic1 head
- 🍽 Cinnamon sticks 1 piece
- 🍽 Thyme 10 stems
- 🍽 Parsley 50 g
- 🍽 Cilantro 20 g
- 🍽 Sea salt 60 g

Instructions:

1. Boil a head of garlic, thyme, cinnamon and star anise cut in half in salt water. Pour the guinea fowl with brine, put in the cold for six hours.

2. In butter, fry the onion with quinoa, then boil. Season with pepper, parsley, cilantro, juice and lime zest.

3. Dry guinea fowl, stuff quinoa.

4. Bake at 190 degrees on a baking sheet greased with vegetable oil, breast up for an hour, periodically pouring with a mixture of wine and oil.

Chicken with Tomatoes, Prunes, Cinnamon and Wine

Servings: 4 | Total Time: 76 mins

Nutrition Information

Calories: 543 | Carbs: 43.3 grams | Fats: 29 grams

Ingredients:

- Ground black pepper to taste
- Chicken 1 piece
- Salt to taste
- Butter 2.5 tablespoons
- White dry wine 250 ml
- Water125 ml
- Tomatoes 250 g
- Cinnamon sticks 1 piece
- Sugar 2 teaspoons
- Pitted prunes 16 pieces
- Red wine vinegar 2 tablespoons

Instructions:

1. Cut the chicken into 8 parts, sprinkle with black pepper and salt.

2. Fry the chicken in butter in a heavy skillet in two batches (5 minutes each).

3. When the roasting process is complete, firmly place all the pieces of chicken in a pan (skin down), add wine, bring to a boil and wait until the liquid has evaporated by half (about 5 minutes).

4. Add water to the pan, add peeled and finely chopped tomatoes, 1 cinnamon stick, 3/4 teaspoon of salt, 1/4 teaspoon of pepper and bring to a boil again. Continue cooking, covered, over low heat for 20 minutes.

5. Add prunes, vinegar and sugar to a frying pan, chopped into large frying pan, bring to a boil again, reduce heat, cover and cook for 10 minutes. Then use forceps to remove the pieces of chicken from the pan, put on a dish and cover with foil.

6. Bring the sauce remaining in the pan to a boil and continue cooking over high heat for 8-10 minutes. Wait until the sauce thickens and evaporates to about 300 ml. Remove the cinnamon stick from the sauce.

7. Put the chicken on plates at the rate of 2 pieces for 1 person. Serve with cooked tomato and prune sauce.

Pork stew with celery, carrots, madeira and spices

Servings: 6 | Total Time: 75 mins

Nutrition Information

Calories: 386 | Carbs: 19.5 grams | Fats: 17 grams

Ingredients:

- Celery stalk 6 pieces
- Pork fillet 900 g
- Onion 2 heads
- Garlic 3 cloves
- Canned Tomatoes 400 g
- Ground black pepper to taste
- Dried thyme ¼ teaspoon
- Salt to taste
- Ground cinnamon ¼ teaspoon
- Ground coriander ¼ teaspoon
- Canned Green Peas 200 g
- Carrot 300 g
- Rosemary ¼ teaspoon
- Juniper berries 1/2 teaspoon
- Madeira wine 125 g
- Bay leaf 2 pieces
- Vegetable oil 2 tablespoons

Instructions:

1. Cut the pork into cubes (2.5-3 cm) and sprinkle with salt and pepper.

2. Peel the carrots, one half of which is cut into large slices, and the other is finely chopped. Chop garlic and onion finely. Cut celery stalks into circles.

3. Heat a large deep frying pan and fry the pork in hot oil, stirring constantly. After about 10-12 minutes, remove the meat and put in a bowl.

4. In the same pan, passer for 5-7 minutes finely chopped vegetables, after draining from the pan almost all the fat. Add spices, juniper berries and continue to passer for another 1 minute.

5. Pour Madeira into sauteed vegetables and bring to a boil while continuing to stir.

6. Return the meat to the pan, add canned tomatoes and large slices of carrots. Bring everything to a boil again and continue cooking over moderate heat, stirring occasionally.

7. After about half an hour, when the liquid thickens and the meat becomes soft, throw peas into the stew, stir and simmer for another 5 minutes.

8. Before serving, remove the bay leaves from the stew and let it brew for at least 15 minutes. It can be boiled potatoes as a side dish.

Turkey thigh pastrami

Servings: 4 | Total Time: 80 mins

Nutrition Information

Calories: 340 | Carbs: 2.3 grams | Fats: 22.8 grams

Ingredients:

- Turkey Thigh 800 g
- Water 2 cups
- Unrefined sunflower oil 1 tablespoon
- Ground paprika 2 teaspoons
- Curry Powder 1 teaspoon
- Ground white and black peppers ½ teaspoon each
- Salt 4.5 tablespoons
- Ground ginger ⅓ teaspoon
- Ground red pepper to taste

Instructions:

1. Rinse the thigh of a turkey well and fill it with brine so that the liquid completely covers the meat (at the rate of 1 tablespoon of salt per 1 cup of water). Refrigerate after covering for overnigh.

2. For marinade, mix sunflower oil, ground paprika, curry, ground white and black pepper, salt to taste and ground ginger.

3. Remove the meat from the solution, dry and grease evenly with marinade.

4. Wrap with a roll, knit with a thread, net or bandage. Place on a baking sheet covered with baking paper or foil.

5. Bake pastrami in the oven, heated to 250 degrees 25 minutes. Turn off the oven and leave the pastrami ready for another 40 minutes. Cool it to the temperature of room.

6. Cut the pastrami into slices and serve.

Lamb with plums

Servings: 4 | Total Time: 135 mins

Nutrition Information
Calories: 904 | Carbs: 31.7 grams | Fats: 68.4 grams

Ingredients:

- 🍽 Lamb 1 kg
- 🍽 Plums 500 g
- 🍽 Onion 1 head
- 🍽 Garlic 1 clove
- 🍽 Olive oil 4 tablespoons
- 🍽 Saffron 1/2 teaspoon
- 🍽 ¼ teaspoon nutmeg
- 🍽 Grated ginger 1/2 teaspoon
- 🍽 Cinnamon 2 teaspoons
- 🍽 Sugar 2 tablespoons
- 🍽 Pine nuts 50 g
- 🍽 Ground black pepper and salt to taste

Instructions:

1. Passer chopped onions in a thick-walled pan in olive oil until golden brown. Put chopped garlic and diced meat there and fry, stirring constantly. Add salt, saffron, ginger, nutmeg. Pour water so that it covers the meat, and simmer under the lid for 1—1, 5 hours.

2. Remove the seeds and cut the plums in half. Put in a pan, add sugar, cinnamon and pepper. Stew, lid for 15 minutes, then another 5 minutes without a lid to thicken the sauce.

3. Put the lamb in a dish and sprinkle lightly with pine nuts (without oil) or chopped almonds.

Meals with fish and seafood

Low-fat fish is used in almost every low-calorie diet for weight loss, as it gives the body plenty of protein and a minimum of fat. In addition, low-fat varieties of fish contain a very small number of calories and thus give the feeling of satiety for a long time.

Octopus with artichoke and tomato-mint sauce

Servings: 1 | Total Time: 40 mins

Nutrition Information

Calories: 898 | Carbs: 37.9 grams | Fats: 51.1 grams

Ingredients:

- Artichokes 1 piece
- Carrot 1 piece
- Tomatoes 3 pieces
- Cherry Tomatoes 3 pieces
- Octopus tentacle 1 piece
- Garlic 1 clove
- Olive oil 50 ml
- Thyme to taste
- Dry white wine 70 ml
- Fresh mint 1 bunch
- Lemon juice 30 ml

Instructions:

1. Cut off the top of the artichoke so that it can be tightly placed on the board. After do the same with hard outer leaves, then remove the fleecy core and several internal purple leaves, cut off the stem. Pour all slices with lemon juice and put in a bowl of cold water.

2. Peel the carrots and cut into small cubes. Blanch the tomatoes in boiling water, then cut and peel two of them in the same way. Next, in the end, slice an artichoke. Put the legs of the octopus in a stew pan, add water and cook on medium heat for 20- 25 minutes.

3. Heat olive oil in and toss artichoke cubes, after add juice of lemon (you can squeeze it directly with your hands from half a lemon slice), fry and mix for a few minutes.

4. Add tomatoes and carrots, black pepper, thyme, salt and chopped garlic to the artichoke, mix and fry all together for another 2 minutes. Then pour the wine. Boil over low heat. .

5. Put the rest of peeled tomato into the blender bowl, add the mint leaves (leaving a few pieces for decoration) and beat until smooth. Take out the cooked octopus in a colander and dry.

6. Fry the octopus in a small frying pan using olive oil on all sides for 3 to 4 minutes until a light golden cover appears.

7. Use 2 tablespoons of the vegetable mixture on each plates, nicely place the toasted octopus tentacle on top of all serving.

8. Pour each serving with a small amount of tomato and mint sauce, and sprinkle with chopped mint leaves on top.

Mediterranean Mussels

Servings: 2 | Total Time: 20 mins

Nutrition Information
Calories: 877 | Carbs: 10.7 grams | Fats: 63.3 grams

Ingredients:

- Mussels 500 g
- Dry white wine 1 cup
- Olive Oil 2 tablespoon
- Onions 1/2 heads
- Garlic 2 cloves
- Cheese 200 g
- Chopped parsley 1 tablespoon
- Cream 200 ml

Instructions:

1. Slightly fry chopped onions and garlic in olive oil. Then put the previously thawed mussels in this mixture, hold them on the fire for a bit and add wine.

2. When the alcohol is half evaporated, add cheese, parsley and black pepper.

3. Wait for the cheese to melt in wine, add cream to the eye, bring them to a boil and remove from heat.

Shrimp with ginger and sherry

Servings: 1 | Total Time: 15 mins

Nutrition Information

Calories: 568 | Carbs: 4.5 grams | Fats: 43.1 grams

Ingredients:

- Peeled Shrimp 150 g
- Butter 2 tablespoons
- Grated ginger 1.5 teaspoons
- Sherry 2 tablespoons
- Cilantro 2 tablespoons
- Salt to taste
- Ground black pepper to taste

Instructions:

1. Wash shrimps in cold running water, dry and sprinkle with salt.

2. In a medium-sized frying pan with a heavy bottom, heat butter over moderate heat. Then throw grated ginger there and saute for 30 seconds.

3. After the ginger, send the shrimp into the pan and fry for 2 minutes.

4. Pour sherry into a pan with shrimp and ginger and continue cooking for another 2 minutes.

5. Add roughly chopped cilantro to the pan, season with salt and pepper and mix.

6. Serve with baguette. As a side dish you can use green beans.

Baked red sea bass with lemon-basil sauce

Servings: 2 | Total Time: 60 mins

Nutrition Information

Calories: 479 | Carbs: 3.5 grams | Fats: 29.6 grams

Ingredients:

- Sea bass 600 g
- Basil leaves1 bunch
- Lemon zest 1 tablespoon
- Lemon juice 1 tablespoon
- Ground pepper
- Garlic 2 cloves
- Olive oil 50 ml
- Salt to taste

Instructions:

1. Clean fish from scales, gut.

2. In a blender mix basil leaves, zest of one lemon, lemon juice, garlic, chili pepper, olive oil, salt.

3. Grease the fish with the mixture.

4. Cover the baking dish with parchment and put the fish on it.

5. Top cover the mold with aluminum foil and bake until the fish breaks up into fibers, if pierced with a fork, 45-50 minutes. Serve hot or warm by pouring out the allocated juice.

Mussels baked with tomatoes, cheese and onions

Servings: 2 | Total Time: 35 mins

Nutrition Information

Calories: 352 | Carbs: 12.5 grams | Fats: 18 grams

Ingredients:

- 🍽 Mussel meat 400 g
- 🍽 Tomatoes 2 pieces
- 🍽 Cheese 100 g
- 🍽 Onion1 piece
- 🍽 Salt to taste
- 🍽 Lemon 1 piece
- 🍽 Dry white wine 50 ml
- 🍽 Ground black pepper to taste

Instructions:

1. Marinate mussels for 10 minutes in wine, lemon juice, salt, pepper to taste.

2. Onions, tomatoes cut into circles, grind the cheese on a grater.

3. We put the pickled mussels on wooden skewers.

4. On the baking sheet we put the foil (taking into account that the mussels will need to be wrapped), and lay the layers of mussels and prepared vegetables. Sprinkle with cheese.

5. Wrap completely in foil and send it to a preheated oven to 180 degrees for 15-20 minutes.

Sea trout with grilled asparagus and lemons

Servings: 4 | Total Time: 30 mins

Nutrition Information

Calories: 466 | Carbs: 8.3 grams | Fats: 29.6 grams

Ingredients:

- Trout fillet 800 g
- Green Asparagus 24 pieces
- Lemon 4 pieces
- Olive oil 100 ml
- Salt to taste
- Ground black pepper to taste
- Paprika 1 teaspoon
- Ground cumin (zira) ½ teaspoon

Instructions:

1. Mix half the olive oil with paprika, salt, pepper and cumin.

2. Grease trout steaks with this mixture (they should turn out 4 pieces of 200 grams each).

3. Cut lemons in half. Peel the asparagus, dip in water (boiled) and cook for 2 minutes, dip in ice water. Grill steaks until tender.

4. Grill lemons, cut down. Sprinkle asparagus with olive oil and grill.

Grilled salmon with red wine and blackberry wings

Servings: 6 | Total Time: 30 mins

Nutrition Information

Calories: 402 | Carbs: 15.2 grams | Fats: 16 grams

Ingredients:

- Dry red wine1 cup
- Blackberry 475 g
- Shallots 1 head
- Sugar 3 tablespoons
- Grated ginger 2 tablespoons
- Butter 1 tablespoon
- Salmon fillet 6 pieces
- Salt to taste
- Ground black pepper to taste

Instructions:

1. Mix wine and 2 cups of berries in a blender, grind until puree. Strain the mashed potatoes through a sieve in a small saucepan. Add chopped shallots, ginger and 2 tablespoons of sugar. Bring to a boil and cook for about 10 minutes, stirring until the volume is reduced to 1 cup. Remove from heat and stir in butter. Add more sugar if desired.

2. Rinse the fish fillet well and pat dry with a paper towel. Wrap the thin edges from the belly of the fish in the center to the main piece so that they do not burn, and secure with toothpicks.

3. Put the fish on a greased grill and fry until cooked for about 8-10 minutes. Arrange the fish in plates, removing the toothpicks, and pour over the warm wings.

Salmon skewers with cherry in rosemary marinade

Servings: 4 | Total Time: 20 mins

Nutrition Information

Calories: 248 | Carbs: 5.8 grams | Fats: 12.9 grams

Ingredients:

- 🍽 Fresh chopped rosemary 2 teaspoons
- 🍽 Extra virgin olive oil 2 teaspoons
- 🍽 Garlic 2 cloves
- 🍽 Coarse salt 1/2 teaspoon
- 🍽 Grated lemon zest 1 teaspoon
- 🍽 Lemon juice 1 teaspoon
- 🍽 Ground black pepper ¼ teaspoon
- 🍽 Salmon Fillet 500 g
- 🍽 Cherry Tomatoes 400 g

Instructions:

1. Mix chopped rosemary, olive oil, chopped garlic, zest and salt and pepper, lemon juice in a bowl. Add the fish, and after you cut into small pieces, you can mix it.

2. On skewers, alternating, put on cherry and pieces of fish.

3. Put on the grill and fry, gently turning over, 4-6 minutes until it will be cooked.

Stingray in citrus juices with ginger

Servings: 4 | Total Time: 30 mins

Nutrition Information

Calories: 253 | Carbs: 15.3 grams | Fats: 3.1 grams

Ingredients:

- Stingray fillet 680 g
- Orange Juice 3 cups
- Lemon zest 1 teaspoon
- Lime juice ½ cup
- Grated ginger 1.5 teaspoons
- Chives to taste
- Lime 1 piece

Instructions:

1. Combine the grated lemon zest, orange and lime juice, and ginger in a saucepan. Bring it to a boil.

2. Put the stingray fillet, reduce heat and cook for 5 minutes. Gently place the slope on serving plates and keep it warm by covering it with foil.

3. Increase the heat again and cook until the sauce has been evaporated by half, for about 10-15 minutes, without closing the lid (the sauce should look like syrup in consistency). Pour over the fish sauce. Serve sprinkled with chives with lime slices.

Vegetables

Here are 5 receipts of using vegetables which are based on the Mediterranean diet

Mediterranean baked vegetable lasagna

Servings: 6 | Total Time: 150 mins

Nutrition Information

Calories: 409 | Carbs: 28 grams | Fats: 27.1 grams

Ingredients:

- Eggplant 1 piece
- Zucchini 2 pieces
- Cherry Tomatoes 450 g
- Fresh red pepper 1 piece
- Ready-made dry lasagna sheets 9 pieces
- Onion 1 head
- Garlic 2 cloves
- Basil leaves 2 tablespoons
- Olive Oil 3 tablespoons
- Seedless olives 50 g
- Capers 1 tablespoon
- Mozzarella Cheese 75 g
- Wheat flour 35 g
- Butter 40 g
- Milk 570 ml
- Bay leaf 1 piece
- Grated Parmesan Cheese 4 tablespoons

🍽 Nutmeg to taste

Instructions:

1. Cut the eggplant and zucchini into cubes. Mix with salt, put in a colander, cover with a plate and put the load. Leave for an hour to stack the juice. Squeeze out the remaining liquid, dry with a towel.

2. Remove the peel from the tomatoes, peel the seeds from the seeds and cut into cubes, onions also cut into cubes.

3. Place tomatoes, cubes of eggplant, zucchini, pepper and onions on a baking sheet, sprinkle with chopped garlic, basil, drizzle with olive oil. Mix everything thoroughly, salt, pepper and bake at 240 degrees, 30–40 minutes, until the edges of the vegetable cubes are browned. Sprinkle the prepared vegetables with chopped olives and capers.

4. For sauce you need to mix flour, butter, milk in a saucepan, put bay leaf, nutmeg, salt and pepper to taste. Cook, over medium heat, stirring constantly, until the sauce boils and thickens. Reduce heat and cook for another 2 minutes. Stir in 3 tablespoons of grated Parmesan.

5. Pour in a quarter of the sauce and put a third of the vegetable mixture. Sprinkle a third of grated mozzarella cheese and cover with a layer of lasagna leaves. Repeat all over, ending with a layer of sauce. Sprinkle the remaining tablespoon of grated Parmesan.

6. Bake at 180 degrees for about 25-30 minutes until golden and crisp.

Mediterranean vegetables

Servings: 4 | Total Time: 50 mins

Nutrition Information

Calories: 494 | Carbs: 124.6 grams | Fats: 7.6 grams

Ingredients:

- Zucchini 2 pieces
- Red onion 1 head
- Pumpkin squash 2 pieces
- Caraway leaves 1 tablespoon
- Balsamic vinegar 2 tablespoons
- Olive oil 1 teaspoon

Instructions:

1. Oven should be preheated to the 200 degrees. Grease a baking sheet with vegetable oil.

2. Cut the vegetables into small pieces diagonally and place on a baking sheet. Pour olive oil and balsamic vinegar, then sprinkle with chopped caraway leaves and mix well. Flatten in a single layer. Salt and pepper.

3. Bake vegetables until soft and browned for about 35 minutes, stirring occasionally.

Warm baked vegetables salad

Servings: 6 | Total Time: 60 mins

Nutrition Information

Calories: 201 | Carbs: 27.1 grams | Fats: 7.2 grams

Ingredients:

- 🍽 Eggplant 3 pieces
- 🍽 Yellow bell pepper 4 pieces
- 🍽 Red bell pepper 4 pieces
- 🍽 Zucchini 2 pieces
- 🍽 Fennel 2 pieces
- 🍽 Red onion 2 heads
- 🍽 Dill 5 sprigs
- 🍽 Parsley 5 sprigs
- 🍽 Cilantro 5 sprigs
- 🍽 4 garlic cloves
- 🍽 Olive Oil 2 tablespoon
- 🍽 Provencal herbs 1 tablespoon
- 🍽 Lemon juice 1 teaspoon
- 🍽 Sea salt ½ teaspoon

Instructions:

1. Cut eggplant lengthwise into eights, put on a baking sheet, slightly sprinkle with olive oil, sprinkle with salt.

2. Bake in a preheated oven (250 ° C) for 20 minutes until golden brown. Transfer to a salad bowl.

3. Reduce oven temperature to 220 ° C. Peel and finely chop the garlic.

4. Remove the seeds from sweet pepper, cut each into eights as well, spread on a baking sheet, drizzle with olive oil, sprinkle with sea salt, half Provence herbs and garlic, and bake in the oven for 10-15 minutes until cooked.

5. Put pepper in a colander to stack excess juice.

6. Thinly zucchini and put on a baking sheet.

7. Cut fennel and red onion into eight slices, add to the zucchini, sprinkle with olive oil, salt and sprinkle with the remaining Provence herbs.

8. Bake in the oven for 8-10 minutes until the fennel is ready, then cool to the temepature of the room.

9. Chop the greens. Put the baked vegetables in a salad bowl to the eggplant, mix, drizzle with apple cider vinegar or lemon juice, sprinkle with herbs.

Fresh Eggplant Caviar

Servings: 10 | Total Time: 40 mins

Nutrition Information

Calories: 109 | Carbs: 7.8 grams | Fats: 8.1 grams

Ingredients:

- Eggplant 4 pieces
- Tomatoes 4 pieces
- Yellow onion 2 heads
- Ground black pepper to taste
- Salt to taste
- olive oil 4 tablespoons

Instructions:

1. Pierce large washed eggplants with a knife in several places with a knife. Bake in the oven, preheated to 200 degrees.

2. Meanwhile, peel and finely chop the onion.

3. Blanch tomatoes (select medium-sized fruits) and peel. Mash in a blender. Add salt, pepper and olive oil there.

4. Peel the eggplants baked until soft and peel off the edges. Grind the inside with a knife.

5. Mix all the ingredients and refrigerate them.

Grilled seafood with vegetables

Servings: 1 | Total Time: 35 mins

Nutrition Information

Calories: 336 | Carbs: 7.8 grams | Fats: 14.8 grams

Ingredients:

- 🍽 Octopus 60 g
- 🍽 Cuttlefish 60 g
- 🍽 Shrimp 60 g
- 🍽 Scallops 60 g
- 🍽 Sweet pepper 50 g
- 🍽 Zucchini 30 g
- 🍽 Eggplant 30 g
- 🍽 Butter 15 g

Instructions:

1. All seafood should be per-processed, greased and fried on birch coals.

2. Vegetables are processed chopped and grilled on charcoal.

3. We spread the cooked seafood and vegetables in a copper preheated pan.

Salads

Here are 5 receipts of fresh salads which are based on the Mediterranean diet

Salad with Asparagus, Eggplant and Feta Cheese

Servings: 4 | Total Time: 40 mins

Nutrition Information

Calories: 272 | Carbs: 18 grams | Fats: 16.9 grams

Ingredients:

- Fresh Asparagus 500 g
- Eggplant 2 pieces
- Leek 4 stems
- Feta Cheese 100 g
- Peeled Pumpkin Seeds 50 g
- Chives1 bunch
- Chili pepper 1 piece
- Olive oil 2 teaspoons
- Salt to taste

Instructions:

1. Heat a little of olive oil in a heavy frying pan and fry the asparagus for 3-4 minutes to make it softer, then darken a couple of minutes under the lid and put in a different bowl.

2. Cut the eggplant in small circles, sprinkle with salt and fry in the same pan (you can not add oil).

3. Simmer and cover for another 10 minutes, then remove the lid and hold the eggplants on the fire for another 5 minutes until they become a smooth golden color.

4. Remove the eggplants from the pan and set aside.

5. Cut the leek into thin rings.

6. Add a little of oil in the same pan and fry the onions over high heat until golden brown, then cover and simmer for 3-4 minutes until the fire is tender, until the onions are soft. Put it in a colander to stack extra juice.

7. Chilli and chives.

8. Cut the cooled asparagus into three parts, combine with leek, chili pepper and eggplant, sprinkle with green onions and pumpkin seeds, pour over the remaining oil.

9. Break the feta into small pieces and sprinkle the salad. Mix everything and serve the salad at room temperature.

Salad with quail eggs, salmon and cherry tomatoes

Servings: 4 | Total Time: 25 mins

Nutrition Information

Calories: 277 | Carbs: 2.8 grams | Fats: 25.9 grams

Ingredients:

- 🍽 Iceberg salad 1 piece
- 🍽 Lightly salted salmon 100 g
- 🍽 Cherry Tomatoes 16 pieces
- 🍽 Quail egg 8 pieces
- 🍽 4 tablespoons olive oil
- 🍽 Parsley 15 g
- 🍽 Lemon juice 1 tablespoon
- 🍽 Salt to taste
- 🍽 Ground black pepper to taste

Instructions:

1. Rinse the salad. Cut the head into small pieces and pat dry on a napkin. Boil the quail egg in boiling water for 3-4 minutes, then immediately transfer to cold water and allow to cool completely. Peel and cut each egg in half.

2. Rinse the cherry tomatoes and, cutting into 4 parts, season with salt. Rinse and dry the parsley.

3. For the sauce in a blender, beat the lemon juice, olive oil and parsley until smooth, season with salt and pepper.

4. Put the salad on a plate. Cut the salmon into thin slices or cubes, put on a salad. Add slices of cherry tomatoes and halves of quail eggs. Garnish with the resulting sauce before serving.

Grilled vegetables salad

Servings: 4 | Total Time: 60 mins

Nutrition Information

Calories: 109 | Carbs: 17.5 grams | Fats: 1.7 grams

Ingredients:

- 🍽 Eggplant 2 pieces
- 🍽 Zucchini 2 pieces
- 🍽 Sweet pepper 2 pieces
- 🍽 Cucumbers 2 pieces
- 🍽 Natural Yogurt 150 g
- 🍽 Garlic 3 cloves
- 🍽 Lemon juice 2 teaspoons
- 🍽 Salt and black pepper to taste

Instructions:

1. Cut eggplant and zucchini into circles.

2. Grease with olive oil, bake on the grill.

3. Cucumber cut into slices, pepper into cubes.

4. Slices of eggplant and zucchini in half.

5. Yogurt mixed with finely chopped garlic and lemon juice.

6. Mix all the vegetables in a bowl, salt and pepper add to taste, pour the dressing.

Shrimp salad with mustard and lemon sauce

Servings: 3 | Total Time: 10 mins

Nutrition Information

Calories: 240 | Carbs: 3.3 grams | Fats: 21.5 grams

Ingredients:

- Boiled peeled king prawns 120 g
- Arugula1 bunch
- Cucumbers 2 pieces
- Lemon 1/2 pieces
- Iceberg salad 1/2 pieces
- Granular mustard 2 teaspoons
- Olive Oil 3 tablespoons

Instructions:

1. Wash and chop all vegetables.

2. Peel the shrimp from its tails, cut into three parts.

3. For the sauce, squeeze half a lemon into a glass, add 2 teaspoons of mustard, then pour 3 tablespoons of olive oil, mix thoroughly.

4. Pour salad dressing and serve.

Salad with tuna and capers

Servings: 2 | Total Time: 15 mins

Nutrition Information

Calories: 89 | Carbs: 5 grams | Fats: 1.1 grams

Ingredients:

- ▌●▐ Green salad 1/2 bunch
- ▌●▐ Canned tuna in its own juice 120 g
- ▌●▐ Cherry Tomatoes 10 pieces
- ▌●▐ Pickled capers 20 g
- ▌●▐ Salt to taste
- ▌●▐ Balsamic to taste
- ▌●▐ Cucumbers 1 piece

Instructions:

1. Tomatoes and cucumber cut into 4 parts, sectors. Break salad, split tuna into small pieces, add capers, salt, mix.

2. Top with balsamic sauce.

Snacks/Desserts

Here are full 2 receipts of low-calorie deserts and small receipts according the Mediterranean diet

1) Cantucci. This is an almond cookie that is made extremely simple, unlike other baked goods with almonds, which are added to the Mediterranean cuisine.

2) Peaches in almonds can be made so that the almonds are laid inside, for this you need to cut a blind hole in the peach, or the peach is divided into two parts, and instead of the stone, the almonds lie. All this is baked.

3) Cheesecake with cottage cheese, Greek yogurt instead of cream, fruits, vanilla, cinnamon and cookies.

4) Semifreddo. As we already know, ice cream is considered the norm in the Mediterranean, of course, in such a heat. Ice cream should be done by yourself or choose the best quality. In the semifreddo recipe, ice cream is served with hazelnuts.

Peach Lime Sorbet

Servings: 4 | Total Time: 30 mins

Nutrition Information

Calories: 213 | Carbs: 53.6 grams | Fats: 0.1 grams

Ingredients:

- 🍽 Water 1.5 cup
- 🍽 Sugar 0.6 cup
- 🍽 Light corn syrup 2 tablespoons
- 🍽 Peaches 500 g
- 🍽 Grated lime zest 1 teaspoon
- 🍽 ¼ teaspoon salt
- 🍽 Lime juice 6 tablespoons

Instructions:

1. Mix water, sugar and corn syrup in a stew pan. Add the peaches cut in half, bring to a boil and cook, lidding, for 10 minutes.

2. Put the peaches in a blender with syrup and add lime zest, lime juice and salt. Beat until smooth. Then refrigerate for several hours.

3. Freeze in an ice cream maker or pour into a container and put into the freezer for about 6 hours, stirring every 45 minutes

Orange sauce

Servings: 6 | Total Time: 20 mins

Nutrition Information

Calories: 201 | Carbs: 46.9 grams | Fats: 0.3 grams

Ingredients:

- 🍽 Lemon 1 piece
- 🍽 Oranges 4 pieces
- 🍽 Sugar 200 g
- 🍽 Potato starch 1 teaspoon
- 🍽 Cointreau 2 tablespoons

Instructions:

1. Squeeze the juice from oranges and cut a thin layer of lemon peel. All together, plus sugar, put in a ladle and put on a slow fire – stir until sugar is completely dissolved.

2. Mix starch with 3 tablespoons of water in a cup. When there are no lumps in the mixture, add it to the ladle with sauce. Cook, stirring finely for next 2 minutes. Remove the dishes from the heat, add liquor, strain into a jug and let cool.

3. Put into the refrigerator. This sauce goes well with baked desserts and ice cream.

Part 3
44 Days Weight Loss Challenge

For many people, going beyond a certain weight range is close in effect to the approach of the end of the world – even if there is nothing dangerous to health: this is the dictates of the canons of beauty. There are some thing you need to avoid. But in general this diet is super easy to follow with not only few days but in whole life.

Here are some prohibited diet foods:

- ✓ Lard and bacon;
- ✓ Sausages;
- ✓ Carbonated drinks;
- ✓ Highly processed foods such as skim milk and refined cereals.

With any diet option, it is important to note that salads, which are very numerous in Mediterranean cuisine, are never seasoned with mayonnaise. Even if it is made at home. Olive oil, balsamic vinegar and lemon juice are used as dressing. All this can be mixed with herbs that can fully reveal their taste and aroma.

The food is so diverse that losing weight will be a fun experiment, and you will want to continue the diet for life. This can really be done, because these products have everything that the body needs and in sufficient quantity. Sometimes go with a diet in favor of a traditional one. And some products in the diet can be replaced by slightly adapting them to the conditions of our country. There are an incredible number of recipes and their variations are also different. So we provide only a general description, combining below the most popular recipes for this cuisine.

	BREAKFAST	LUNCH	DINNER
DAY 1	Delicate omelet with toast by Gordon Ramsay	Mussels baked with tomatoes, cheese and onions	Spaghetti with anchovies and bread crumbs
DAY 2	Pate with smoked salmon and dill	Shrimp Pumpkin Cream Soup	Grilled seafood with vegetables
DAY 3	Potato salad without mayonnaise	Spaghetti with seafood and cherry tomatoes	Octopus with artichoke and tomato-mint sauce
DAY 4	Fruit and nut granola	Mediterranean Mussels	Homemade Buziate Pasta with Pesto Alla Trapanese
DAY 5	Frittata with broccoli and sweet pepper	Salmon skewers with cherry in rosemary marinade	Risotto with mussels and shrimp
DAY 6	Fruit and nut granola	Sea trout with grilled asparagus and lemons	Potato gratin
DAY 7	Salad with tuna and capers	Barley Risotto	Lamb with plums
DAY 8	Delicate omelet with toast by Gordon Ramsay	Lentil Soup	Perlotto with Rapana
DAY 9	Pate with smoked salmon and dill	Warm baked vegetables salad	Croatian Soup

	BREAKFAST	LUNCH	DINNER
DAY 10	Quick bean salad	Potato and Tuna Casserole	Baked red sea bass with lemon-basil sauce
DAY 11	Fruit and nut granola	Lentils in Tomato Sauce	Spaghetti with seafood and cherry tomatoes
DAY 12	Couscous with pesto	Salad with Asparagus, Eggplant and Feta Cheese	Grilled seafood with vegetables
DAY 13	Frittata with broccoli and sweet pepper	Tuna Ratatouille	Spaghetti with anchovies and bread crumbs
DAY 14	Fruit and nut granola	Sea trout with grilled asparagus and lemons	Risotto with mussels and shrimp
DAY 15	Delicate omelet with toast by Gordon Ramsay	Spaghetti with seafood and cherry tomatoes	Pisto
DAY 16	Fruit and nut granola	Warm baked vegetables salad	Grilled salmon with red wine and blackberry wings
DAY 17	Pate with smoked salmon and dill	Lentil Soup	Homemade Buziate Pasta with Pesto Alla Trapanese
DAY 18	Potato salad without mayonnaise	Barley Risotto	Chicken with Tomatoes, Prunes, Cinnamon and Wine

	BREAKFAST	LUNCH	DINNER
DAY 19	Fruit and nut granola	Salmon skewers with cherry in rosemary marinade	Potato gratin
DAY 20	Frittata with broccoli and sweet pepper	Shrimp Pumpkin Cream Soup	Perlotto with Rapana
DAY 21	Fruit breakfast with nuts	Mediterranean Mussels	Parmigiano Eggplant
DAY 22	Delicate omelet with toast by Gordon Ramsay	Potato and Tuna Casserole	Grilled seafood with vegetables
DAY 23	Pate with smoked salmon and dill	Lentil Soup	Octopus with artichoke and tomato-mint sauce
DAY 24	Quick bean salad	Tuna Ratatouille	Baked red sea bass with lemon-basil sauce
DAY 25	Couscous with pesto	Shrimp with ginger and sherry	Risotto with mussels and shrimp
DAY 26	Fruit and nut granola	Potato salad without mayonnaise	Grilled seafood with vegetables
DAY 27	Frittata with broccoli and sweet pepper	Stingray in citrus juices with ginger	Spaghetti with seafood and cherry tomatoes

	BREAKFAST	LUNCH	DINNER
DAY 28	Fruit and nut granola	Shrimp Pumpkin Cream Soup	Homemade Buziate Pasta with Pesto Alla Trapanese
DAY 29	Delicate omelet with toast by Gordon Ramsay	Lentils in Tomato Sauce	Grilled salmon with red wine and blackberry wings
DAY 30	Pate with smoked salmon and dill	Warm baked vegetables salad	Spaghetti with anchovies and bread crumbs
DAY 31	Fruit breakfast with nuts	Salmon skewers with cherry in rosemary marinade	Pisto
DAY 32	Quick bean salad	Barley Risotto	Guinea fowl with spicy quinoa pilaf
DAY 33	Couscous with pesto	Mediterranean Mussels	Perlotto with Rapana
DAY 34	Salad with Asparagus, Eggplant and Feta Cheese	Spaghetti with seafood and cherry tomatoes	Croatian Soup
DAY 35	Delicate omelet with toast by Gordon Ramsay	Sea trout with grilled asparagus and lemons	Grilled seafood with vegetables
DAY 36	Potato salad without mayonnaise	Tuna Ratatouille	Turkey thigh pastrami

	BREAKFAST	LUNCH	DINNER
DAY 37	Fruit and nut granola	Shrimp with ginger and sherry	Parmigiano Eggplant
DAY 38	Frittata with broccoli and sweet pepper	Salad with tuna and capers	Homemade Buziate Pasta with Pesto Alla Trapanese
DAY 39	Fruit and nut granola	Mussels baked with tomatoes, cheese and onions	Risotto with mussels and shrimp
DAY 40	Pate with smoked salmon and dill	Lentil Soup	Grilled seafood with vegetables
DAY 41	Lentils in Tomato Sauce	Stingray in citrus juices with ginger	Baked red sea bass with lemon-basil sauce
DAY 42	Fruit breakfast with nuts	Spaghetti with seafood and cherry tomatoes	Pisto
DAY 43	Salad with Asparagus, Eggplant and Feta Cheese	Shrimp Pumpkin Cream Soup	Perlotto with Rapana
DAY 44	Couscous with pesto	Salmon skewers with cherry in rosemary marinade	Pork stew with celery, carrots, madeira and spices

Additional receipts for 44 Days Weight Loss Challenge

Quick bean salad

Servings: 2 | Total Time: 10 mins

Nutrition Information

Calories: 477 | Carbs: 57.5 grams | Fats: 20.8 grams

Ingredients:

- Olive Oil 2 tablespoons
- Salt and pepper to taste
- White canned beans 200 g
- Red canned beans 200 g
- Celery Stalk 2 Stems
- Parsley 3 stalks
- Fresh rosemary 1 stem
- Apple cider vinegar 2 tablespoons
- Sugar 2 tablespoons
- Red onion 1/2 pieces

Instructions:

1. Cut the celery stalk into small pieces.

2. Chop red onion and herbs.

3. Mix these ingredients with both types of beans.

4. Separately, beat together vinegar, sugar, olive oil, salt and pepper. Dress the salad with the resulting sauce.

5. Put the salad for cooling, so that the beans absorb the dressing.

Potato salad without mayonnaise

Servings: 4 | Total Time: 60 mins

Nutrition Information
Calories: 190 | Carbs: 30.9 grams | Fats: 6.3 grams

Ingredients:

- Potato 6 pieces
- Chives 4 stems
- Olive oil 1 tablespoon
- Gherkins 60 g
- Granular mustard 1 tablespoon
- Vinegar ¼ cup
- Sugar 1 teaspoon
- Salt ¼ teaspoon
- Ground black pepper ¼ teaspoon

Instructions:

1. Peel the potatoes and chop it. Transfer to a pan and pour water so that it completely covers it, then bring to a boil. Reduce heat and simmer until soft for about 20 minutes. Drain and rinse the potatoes under a stream of cold water to cool.

2. Whisk the mustard, vinegar, salt, olive oil and pepper with a whisk in a large bowl.

3. Add cooled potatoes, chives and gherkins.

4. Stir and refrigerate until serving time.

Spaghetti with seafood and cherry tomatoes

Servings: 2 | Total Time: 30 mins

Nutrition Information

Calories: 343 | Carbs: 39.3 grams | Fats: 11.4 grams

Ingredients:

- 🍽 Spaghetti100 g
- 🍽 Seafood Cocktail 150 g
- 🍽 Cherry Tomatoes 8 pieces
- 🍽 Olive oil 1 tablespoon
- 🍽 Dry red wine to taste
- 🍽 Basil to taste
- 🍽 Garlic 1 clove
- 🍽 Freshly ground black pepper to taste
- 🍽 Salt to taste

Instructions:

1. Put water for spaghetti.

2. Cut tge garlic head in half. Each tomato need to be similary cut into 2 halves. Heat oil in a pan and toss the garlic. Add the tomatoes and let the oil soak its taste. For some time, simmer over low heat until the tomatoes become softly lethargic. Catch the garlic.

3. Meanwhile, put the spaghetti in ready water and bring to a state of "al dente".

4. Mix seafood to tomatoes. If the cans are in oil, then let it drain, otherwise the fish oil will clog olive with its smell. After that, allow the mass to dry over high heat, but do not over dry and do not cover it. Octopuses must be with a golden crust.

5. Catch the pasta from the pan with a special ladle with a hole and add to the seafood sauce. Pour in the wine. Let it boil. Sprinkle with dry basil.

Lentil Soup

Servings: 6 | Total Time: 30 mins

Nutrition Information

Calories: 202 | Carbs: 33.8 grams | Fats: 0.7 grams

Ingredients:

- 🍽 Red lentils 300 g
- 🍽 Onion 1 head
- 🍽 Tomatoes 1 piece
- 🍽 Carrot 2 pieces
- 🍽 Garlic 2 cloves
- 🍽 White bread 3 slices
- 🍽 Ginger Root 10 g
- 🍽 Salt to taste
- 🍽 Ground black pepper to taste

Instructions:

1. Boil lentils.

2. Onions and tomatoes coarsely chopped.

3. Grate the carrots coarsely. Ginger – finely.

4. Chop the garlic.

5. Fry all vegetables in a pan.

6. Add the lentils to the pan.

7. Simmer for 10-15 minutes.

8. Grind everything with a blender.

9. Bread cut into small cubes and fry without oil in a pan over low heat for 10 minutes, constantly stirring.

Shrimp Pumpkin Cream Soup

Servings: 2 | Total Time: 30 mins

Nutrition Information

Calories: 312 | Carbs: 39.3 grams | Fats: 15.2 grams

Ingredients:

- 🍽 Pumpkin 1/2
- 🍽 pieces
- 🍽 Cream 20% 200 ml
- 🍽 Salt to taste
- 🍽 Tiger prawns 10 pieces
- 🍽 Garlic 3 cloves
- 🍽 Ground black pepper to taste
- 🍽 Butter 50 g
- 🍽 Green to taste

Instructions:

1. Cut the pumpkin into pieces 2x2 cm. Cook until soft, add herbs and garlic. After the pumpkin is ready, grind it to a puree state (I use a hand blender – faster and more efficient), add cream and put on low heat for a few minutes.

2. At this moment, in butter with garlic, we fry the shrimp for literally a few minutes until the shrimp turns pink and covered with a little blush.

3. Put the shrimp in a plate, pour the soup on top.

Spaghetti with anchovies and bread crumbs

Servings: 8 | Total Time: 50 mins

Nutrition Information

Calories: 366 | Carbs: 16.7 grams | Fats: 45.4 grams

Ingredients:

- 🍽 Spaghetti 450 g
- 🍽 Canned anchovy fillet 12 pieces
- 🍽 Extra Virgin Olive Oil 125 ml
- 🍽 Garlic 6 cloves
- 🍽 Red chili pepper 1 piece
- 🍽 Parsley 30 g
- 🍽 Bread crumbs 30 g
- 🍽 Salt to taste
- 🍽 Ground black pepper to taste

Instructions:

1. Remove the anchovy fillet from the jar, drain the excess oil, then chop six pieces with a sharp knife to a puree condition and cut the remaining six into 4-5 parts; set aside.

2. Peel the chili seeds and grind.

3. Heat olive oil in a large frying pan, add chopped garlic, chopped anchovies and chili peppers. Put it out together over low heat until the anchovies are almost completely dissolved. Then add chopped parsley and the remaining anchovies, mix and turn off the burner.

4. Cook spaghetti in a large amount of salted water until cooked. As soon as the pasta is ready, fill the glass in which it was brewed and set aside.

5. Discard the spaghetti in a colander, dry and add to the pan to the anchovies. Stir, adding a little water from the paste, if the sauce seems too thick. Then add the bread crumbs, leaving about two tablespoons for serving, mix too, but not too diligently to maintain the texture of the crumbs.

6. Arrange the spaghetti in plates, sprinkle on top each serving with the remaining breadcrumbs

Potato and Tuna Casserole

Servings: 6 | Total Time: 40 mins

Nutrition Information

Calories: 243 | Carbs: 33.2 grams | Fats: 5.3 grams

Ingredients:

- 🍽 Canned Tuna 300 g
- 🍽 Potato1 kg
- 🍽 Onion 1 head
- 🍽 Anchovies 10 g
- 🍽 Thyme 2 stems
- 🍽 Cream100 ml
- 🍽 Gruyere cheese 50 g
- 🍽 Chopped Parsley 5 g
- 🍽 Salt and pepper to taste

Instructions:

1. Peel and boil potatoes in salted water until tender. Part of the water remaining after cooking, save for mashed potatoes. Crush or grind the potatoes in a vegetable mill, add cream and beat them with a whisk until mashed. If it's too steep, add potato broth. Salt, pepper to taste.

2. Chop the onion into thin half rings and darken in olive oil with chopped anchovies and thyme until the onion is caramelized.

3. Mix onion with finely chopped tuna and finely chopped parsley. Spice up.

4. Oil one large form or several small molds, put a mixture of tuna, mashed potato on top. Sprinkle with grated cheese and put in the oven for 15–20 minutes.

Lentils in Tomato Sauce

Servings: 2 | Total Time: 30 mins

Nutrition Information

Calories: 321 | Carbs: 38.2 grams | Fats: 13.7 grams

Ingredients:

- 🍽 Green French Lentils 200 g
- 🍽 4 garlic cloves
- 🍽 Water6 cups
- 🍽 Extra virgin olive oil2 tablespoons
- 🍽 Cherry Tomatoes 250 g
- 🍽 Tomato Sauce1 cup
- 🍽 Sugar 2 teaspoons
- 🍽 Salt to taste
- 🍽 Ground black pepper to taste
- 🍽 Onion1 piece

Instructions:

1. Start by cooking lentils. Thinly chop the garlic and fry in 1 tablespoon of olive oil over low heat. As soon as it becomes golden (namely golden, not brownish), add lentils, add water, add a pinch of salt, then bring to a boil and, reducing the heat to medium-low and cook for another 25 minutes, or until the lentils are soft, but all still will keep in shape.

2. For tomato sauce, chop finely the onion, heat the remaining olive oil over medium heat and fry the onion until soft. Add the cherry tomatoes, cut in half, and cook until the tomato juice turns the onion light red.

3. Add tomato sauce, sugar, salt and pepper. Leave on low heat for 15–20 minutes, stirring occasionally. If the mixture begins to dry, add water.

4. Add lentils to the sauce. Stir and add salt and pepper to taste. Before serving, you can sprinkle with peeled sunflower seeds.

Couscous with pesto

Servings: 4 | Total Time: 20 mins

Nutrition Information

Calories: 112 | Carbs: 8.1 grams | Fats: 7.5 grams

Ingredients:

- 🍽 Couscous 80 g
- 🍽 Pesto 50 g
- 🍽 Tomatoes 50 g
- 🍽 Sun-dried tomatoes 20 g
- 🍽 Hazelnuts 10 g
- 🍽 Watercress 2 g

Instructions:

1. Brew couscous with boiling water and leave for 15 minutes under a closed lid.

2. Cut tomatoes into cubes and hazelnuts into half.

3. Add pesto to couscous and mix it with tomatoes, then put it on a plate.

4. Garnish with sun-dried tomatoes, watercress and hazelnuts.

Grilled seafood with vegetables

Servings: 1 | Total Time: 35 mins

Nutrition Information

Calories: 336 | Carbs: 7.8 grams | Fats: 14.8 grams

Ingredients:

- 🍽 Octopus 60 g
- 🍽 Cuttlefish 60 g
- 🍽 Shrimp 60 g
- 🍽 Scallops 60 g
- 🍽 Sweet pepper 50 g
- 🍽 Zucchini 30 g
- 🍽 Eggplant 30 g
- 🍽 Butter 15 g
- 🍽 Salt to taste
- 🍽 Ground black pepper to taste

Instructions:

1. All seafood is pre-processed, oiled and fried on birch coals.

2. Vegetables are processed cut and grilled on charcoal.

3. Spread the cooked seafood and vegetables in a copper preheated pan, decorate with lemon and herbs.

Homemade Buziate Pasta with Pesto Alla Trapanese

Servings: 8 | Total Time: 90 mins

Nutrition Information

Calories: 620 | Carbs: 63.5 grams | Fats: 33.1 grams

Ingredients:

- Cherry Tomatoes 600 g
- Toasted almonds 150 g
- Basil 50 g
- Grated Parmesan Cheese 90 g
- Extra virgin olive oil 120 ml
- Light raisins 2 tablespoons
- Capers 2 tablespoons
- Chili pepper flakes
- Canned anchovy fillet 3 pieces
- Garlic 2 cloves
- Wheat flour 3 cups
- Chicken egg 3 pieces
- Egg yolk 1 piece
- Salt to taste
- Ground black pepper to taste

Instructions:

1. Beat the tomatoes in a combine to the puree, put in a sieve and strain the juice. Return to the combine, add basil, Parmesan, five tablespoons of oil, raisins, capers, chili, anchovies, chopped garlic and almonds. Punch into a paste, add salt and pepper, refrigerate.

2. Mix the flour with a teaspoon of salt, the remaining oil, eggs, yolk (previously separated from the protein) and two tablespoons of water. Knead the dough for eight minutes, wrap in a film and leave for an hour.

3. Divide into six equal parts, each rolled into a sausage 3 mm thick. Cut into pieces 5 cm long. Each piece in turn is wound on a wooden skewer so that a spiral is obtained, and removed from the skewer.

4. Cook the pasta for 8 minutes. Tilt in a colander, then mix in a large bowl with pesto and arrange on plates.

Perlotto with Rapana

Servings: 2 | Total Time: 45 mins

Nutrition Information

Calories: 801 | Carbs: 70.2 grams | Fats: 39.9 grams

Ingredients:

- Champignons600 g
- Shallots120 g
- Rapana 400 g
- Garlic45 g
- Dried Thyme 6 g
- Olive oil90 ml
- Butter90 g
- Cream 35% 150 ml
- Truffle Oil30 ml
- Cognac 180 g
- Fish broth 1 l
- Dried parsley 30 g
- Mushroom broth 500 ml
- Pearl barley 500 g
- Salt to taste
- Ground black pepper to taste
- Green to taste

Instructions:

1. Soak the pearl barley for 3-4 hours, and in the meantime thaw the raspans in the refrigerator. Then cook in salted fish broth: throw into boiling, let it boil a second time, reduce the temperature and cook for 2-3 minutes.

2. Put the clam meat in a colander and pour over cold water. When cooled, cut into four parts. Finely chop the shallots, garlic and parsley.

3. Heat olive oil in a deep skillet. Saute garlic and shallots. Add champignons and evaporate all the water. Add cognac and evaporate alcohol.

4. Add barley and darken, stirring, for a couple of minutes.

5. Start one ladle to pour mushroom broth, as in a risotto. Add the next portion of the liquid when the previous one has already been absorbed. Thus bring the perlotto to readiness (about 25 minutes).

6. When the perlotto is almost ready, heat the butter in a small skillet and quickly fry the clams in it. Add thyme, parsley, cream, salt, pepper, truffle oil to the perlotto; mix vigorously and immediately remove from heat. Arrange in warm plates. Put slices of rape on top and garnish with watercress and sun-dried tomatoes.

Risotto with mussels and shrimp

Servings: 4 | Total Time: 20 mins

Nutrition Information

Calories: 720 | Carbs: 90.9 grams | Fats: 20.7 grams

Ingredients:

- 🍽 Rice 400 g
- 🍽 Mussels 500 g
- 🍽 Shrimp 300 g
- 🍽 Red onion 1/2 heads
- 🍽 Bay leaf 1 piece
- 🍽 Parsley 20 g
- 🍽 Dry Martini 50 ml
- 🍽 Dry white wine 200 ml
- 🍽 Vegetable broth 1.5 l
- 🍽 Tomatoes 200 g
- 🍽 Olive oil 50 ml
- 🍽 Butter 20 g
- 🍽 Lemon1 piece
- 🍽 Thyme 1 piece
- 🍽 Black pepper peas 5 pieces
- 🍽 Ground white pepper and salt to taste

Instructions:

1. Fry the onions with butter in a saucepan until soft. Pour a glass of wine into a saucepan, toss a sprig of black peppercorns, thyme, bay leaf and pour mussels. Salt the mussels if they are not fresh..

2. Cover the pan with a lid and cook the contents over medium heat until the mussels open – for about three minutes. As soon as the mussels open, throw to them in the company, peeled shrimps, pepper, chopped tomatoes and parsley, stir and remove from heat.

3. Heat the olive oil and fry the rice on it so that it is saturated with oil, and pour a third of the available broth into the stew pan.

4. Once the broth boils, lower the temperature and cook, stirring constantly and adding the broth as it boils. Together with one of the injections of the broth, you need to pour a glass of martini. When the rice is almost ready, it must be salted.

5. Then add a pinch of parsley, juice of lemon and dump everything from the pan - mussels, shrimp and onions, along with the broth, in which all this was cooked. Mix gently and immediately remove from heat.

Barley Risotto

Servings: 8 | Total Time: 35 mins

Nutrition Information

Calories: 197 | Carbs: 33.4 grams | Fats: 4.9 grams

Ingredients:

- Pearl barley 450 g
- Orange zest 1 teaspoon
- Chicken stock 400 ml
- Thyme1 stem
- Butter 30 g
- Grated Parmesan Cheese 60 g
- Salt to taste
- Ground black pepper to taste

Instructions:

1. Cook the barley in salted water until half cooked, for twenty to twenty-five minutes. Fold in a colander and rinse with cold water so that the cereal is not prepared by internal heat.

2. Transfer the barley to a large stew pan, add the broth, fresh zest and finely chopped thyme leaves. Simmer on low heat, stirring constantly, until the whole broth is absorbed – it takes about five minutes.

3. Stir in butter and grated Parmesan in the risotto, salt and pepper to taste – and serve that hot.

Potato gratin

Servings: 4 | Total Time: 30 mins

Nutrition Information

Calories: 380 | Carbs: 30.3 grams | Fats: 27.4 grams

Ingredients:

- Potato 6 pieces
- Cream 30% 250 ml
- Garlic 1 clove
- Butter 30 g
- Nutmeg
- Salt to taste
- Ground black pepper to taste
- Cheese to taste

Instructions:

1. Grate the pan inside with a clove of garlic and butter.

2. Cut the potatoes into thin round slices and lay in layers in a mold, sprinkled with salt and pepper.

3. Pour in the cream.

4. Sprinkle with nutmeg and slices of oil.

5. Bake at 200 degrees until cooked.

Tuna Ratatouille

Servings: 6 | Total Time: 90 mins

Nutrition Information

Calories: 295 | Carbs: 17.5 grams | Fats: 21.1 grams

Ingredients:

- 🍽 Canned tuna in its own juice 200 g
- 🍽 Tomatoes 750 g
- 🍽 Onion 2 pieces
- 🍽 Green pepper 1 piece
- 🍽 Zucchini1.5 kg
- 🍽 Olive oil 120 ml

Instructions:

1. Chop the onion. Peel the zucchini from the skin and seeds, chop finely. Remove the seeds from the peppers and cut them into cubes too. Take away the skin and finely chop. Mash tuna with a fork.

2. Heat 4 tablespoons of olive oil in a large bowl. Add the zucchini and cook, stirring occasionally, for 2-3 minutes, then add 3 tablespoons of water and cook another 15 minutes until they become soft.

3. Heat 3 tablespoons of the remaining olive oil in a not big skillet. Pour pepper, cover and cook over low heat, stirring occasionally, for 15 minutes. Remove the slotted spoon from the pan and set aside. Add onions to this skillet and cook over low heat, stirring for 10 minutes, until it turns golden. Add the tomatoes and cook, crushing them with a spatula, for another 15-20 minutes: until the mixture becomes like a sauce.

4. Transfer the tomatoes and onions into the zucchini pan, mix the peppers and cook, stirring, for another 10 minutes. Add tuna, mix and serve.

Pisto

The Pisto is a Spanish version of ratatouille and shakshuks at the same time: first stew the vegetables, and then break the eggs into them so that the yolk remains intact. If you can cook it without eggs, then the pisto will be served with bread.

Servings: 4 | Total Time: 60 mins

Nutrition Information
Calories: 428 | Carbs: 27.8 grams | Fats: 29.5 grams

Ingredients:

🍽️ Zucchini 2 pieces

🍽️ Eggplant 1 piece

🍽️ Sweet pepper 3 pieces

🍽️ Onion 3 heads

🍽️ Canned Tomatoes 400 g

🍽️ Garlic 3 cloves

🍽️ Dried thyme to taste

🍽️ Dried Rosemary to taste

🍽️ Olive oil 90 ml

🍽️ Chicken egg 4 pieces

🍽️ Sugar to taste

🍽️ Salt to taste

🍽️ Ground black pepper to taste

Instructions:

1. Cut the eggplant into small cubes, put on towels (you can use paper one), salt and let it stay for 10 minutes.

2. Cut the remaining vegetables in the same way as eggplant. Heat olive oil in a pan, fry onions and peppers until soft for 12-14 minutes over medium heat. Then add chopped garlic, fry for 30 seconds and add tomatoes, thyme and rosemary, mix and leave over medium heat for 10 minutes.

3. Fry the eggplant in a little amount of olive oil for 4–5 minutes in separate pan. Place eggplant in a clean bowl. Fry zucchini in the same pan, also 4-5 minutes.

4. Add the fried zucchini and eggplant to the vegetables, mix, cover and simmer for 20 minutes.

5. Add salt, sugar and pepper to taste, mix, make indentations in the vegetable mass and break the eggs into them so that the yolk remains intact. Cook and cover for another 4–5 minutes until the protein sets.

Croatian Soup

Servings: 8 | Total Time: 35 mins

Nutrition Information

Calories: 406 | Carbs: 10.9 grams | Fats: 35.4 grams

Ingredients:

- Tomatoes 5 pieces
- Parsley 2 bunches
- Onion1 piece
- Garlic 1 clove
- Feta cheese 200 g
- White crackers to taste
- 5 tablespoons olive oil
- Salt to taste
- Ground black pepper to taste

Instructions:

1. Cut the feta cheese into large cubes and add water for 10-15 minutes to wash the excess salt. If it is not very salty, then you can not do this.

2. You need to prepare all the vegetables first. Parsley should be a big bunch and a little bit (to then add more to the soup fresh). Finely chop onion, garlic, parsley. Cut the tomatoes with a cross, pour boiling water for 1 minute, peel and chop into small pieces. Number of tomatoes – to taste. So that the soup does not turn out to be "empty", chopped tomatoes in volume should be approximately 1 / 5–1 / 4 of the pan.

3. Heat olive oil in a saucepan (so that a couple of mm covers the bottom), fry the onion and garlic a little, add parsley, fry for 2-3 minutes, stirring. After that add the tomatoes, hold for a couple of minutes over high heat, then add half a glass of water or vegetable broth, lower the heat, cover and simmer for 15–20 minutes.

4. When everything is stewed and the tomatoes become almost homogeneous, add water or broth to the required consistency of soup, bring to a boil. Throw the washed feta cheese, cook for about 5 minutes. If the feta cheese starts to melt treacherously (sometimes such feta cheese comes across) - very quickly remove from heat.

Parmigiano Eggplant

Servings: 6 | Total Time: 120 mins

Nutrition Information
Calories: 471 | Carbs: 13.8 grams | Fats: 40.3 grams

Ingredients:

- Eggplant 1 kg
- Vegetable oil 100 ml
- Olive oil 40 ml
- Garlic 1 clove
- Canned Tomatoes 1 kg
- Mozzarella Cheese 300 g
- Grated Parmesan Cheese 100 g
- Basil 10 g
- Salt to taste
- Ground black pepper to taste

Instructions:

1. Cut the eggplant into slices about a centimeter thick. Lay them in layers in a large container, salting each layer. Leave for an hour. Then rinse and dry on paper towels.

2. Heat the vegetable oil and fry the eggplant on it on both sides until golden brown. Put the finished eggplant on paper towels.

3. Heat olive oil in a saucepan, fry chopped garlic for 30 seconds, then add tomatoes and chopped basil. Simmer for 5–7 minutes until the tomatoes are soft. Add salt and pepper to taste.

4. Grease the baking dish with olive oil, put a layer of eggplant, grease with sauce, then put mozzarella and Parmesan. Repeat two more times, finish with a layer of Parmesan. Put in the oven, preheated to 180 degrees, for 40 minutes.

Disclaimer

The opinions and ideas of the author contained in this publication are designed to educate the reader in an informative and helpful manner. While we accept that the instructions will not suit every reader, it is only to be expected that the recipes might not gel with everyone. Use the book responsibly and at your own risk. This work with all its contents, does not guarantee correctness, completion, quality or correctness of the provided information. Always check with your medical practitioner should you be unsure whether to follow a low carb eating plan. Misinformation or misprints cannot be completely eliminated. Human error is real!

Cover: NataliaDesign

Cover Photo: Kiian Oksana // shutterstock.com

Printed in Great Britain
by Amazon

44535871R00066